FRACTION INTERACTIONS

Math 5th Grade
Children's Math Books

BABY PROFESSOR
EDUCATION KIDS

HI KIDS!

Let's practice adding and
subtracting fractions.

Find the sum and shade the figure with the indicated fraction.

1) $\dfrac{1}{9}$ + $\dfrac{1}{9}$ = $\dfrac{2}{9}$

2) $\dfrac{1}{10}$ + $\dfrac{5}{10}$ = ___

3) $\dfrac{1}{5}$ + $\dfrac{3}{5}$ = ___

4) $\dfrac{1}{6}$ + $\dfrac{2}{6}$ = ___

5) $\dfrac{1}{8}$ + $\dfrac{5}{8}$ = ___

1)

$\frac{3}{12}$ + $\frac{8}{12}$ = _____

2)

$\frac{1}{7}$ + $\frac{4}{7}$ = _____

3)

$\frac{1}{8}$ + $\frac{5}{8}$ = _____

4)

$\frac{2}{6}$ + $\frac{2}{6}$ = _____

5)

$\frac{1}{11}$ + $\frac{6}{11}$ = _____

Find the sum and shade the figure with the indicated fraction.

1) $\dfrac{2}{11}$ + $\dfrac{7}{11}$ = _____

2) $\dfrac{1}{3}$ + $\dfrac{1}{3}$ = _____

3) $\dfrac{2}{12}$ + $\dfrac{6}{12}$ = _____

4) $\dfrac{4}{11}$ + $\dfrac{6}{11}$ = _____

5) $\dfrac{1}{10}$ + $\dfrac{1}{10}$ = _____

Find the sum and shade the figure with the indicated fraction.

1)

$$\frac{3}{11} + \frac{5}{11} = \underline{\qquad}$$

2)

$$\frac{2}{6} + \frac{3}{6} = \underline{\qquad}$$

3)

$$\frac{1}{11} + \frac{4}{11} = \underline{\qquad}$$

4)

$$\frac{1}{9} + \frac{5}{9} = \underline{\qquad}$$

5)

$$\frac{3}{7} + \frac{3}{7} = \underline{\qquad}$$

**Find the sum and shade the figure
with the indicated fraction.**

1)

$$\frac{2}{10} + \frac{2}{10} = \underline{\quad\quad}$$

2)

$$\frac{1}{4} + \frac{2}{4} = \underline{\quad\quad}$$

3)

$$\frac{1}{3} + \frac{1}{3} = \underline{\quad\quad}$$

4)

$$\frac{2}{12} + \frac{4}{12} = \underline{\quad\quad}$$

5)

$$\frac{2}{9} + \frac{2}{9} = \underline{\quad\quad}$$

Find the sum.

1) $\dfrac{1}{10} + \dfrac{6}{10} = \dfrac{7}{10}$

2) $\dfrac{2}{7} + \dfrac{2}{7} =$

3) $\dfrac{2}{11} + \dfrac{4}{11} =$

4) $\dfrac{1}{5} + \dfrac{3}{5} =$

5) $\dfrac{2}{12} + \dfrac{8}{12} =$

6) $\dfrac{1}{4} + \dfrac{2}{4} =$

7) $\dfrac{4}{12} + \dfrac{6}{12} =$

8) $\dfrac{3}{10} + \dfrac{3}{10} =$

9) $\dfrac{1}{9} + \dfrac{4}{9} =$

10) $\dfrac{1}{6} + \dfrac{3}{6} =$

Find the sum.

1) $\dfrac{2}{12} + \dfrac{5}{12} =$

2) $\dfrac{1}{10} + \dfrac{6}{10} =$

3) $\dfrac{3}{10} + \dfrac{6}{10} =$

4) $\dfrac{3}{12} + \dfrac{5}{12} =$

5) $\dfrac{1}{4} + \dfrac{1}{4} =$

6) $\dfrac{1}{5} + \dfrac{1}{5} =$

7) $\dfrac{4}{11} + \dfrac{5}{11} =$

8) $\dfrac{1}{7} + \dfrac{3}{7} =$

9) $\dfrac{1}{9} + \dfrac{2}{9} =$

10) $\dfrac{1}{3} + \dfrac{1}{3} =$

Find the sum.

1) $\dfrac{1}{11} + \dfrac{2}{11} =$

2) $\dfrac{1}{9} + \dfrac{6}{9} =$

3) $\dfrac{1}{7} + \dfrac{2}{7} =$

4) $\dfrac{1}{3} + \dfrac{1}{3} =$

5) $\dfrac{2}{12} + \dfrac{4}{12} =$

6) $\dfrac{4}{12} + \dfrac{7}{12} =$

7) $\dfrac{1}{8} + \dfrac{6}{8} =$

8) $\dfrac{1}{5} + \dfrac{2}{5} =$

9) $\dfrac{1}{10} + \dfrac{2}{10} =$

10) $\dfrac{1}{6} + \dfrac{3}{6} =$

Find the sum.

1) $\dfrac{3}{12} + \dfrac{8}{12} =$

2) $\dfrac{1}{3} + \dfrac{1}{3} =$

3) $\dfrac{2}{8} + \dfrac{3}{8} =$

4) $\dfrac{1}{6} + \dfrac{3}{6} =$

5) $\dfrac{2}{5} + \dfrac{2}{5} =$

6) $\dfrac{1}{7} + \dfrac{5}{7} =$

7) $\dfrac{1}{11} + \dfrac{3}{11} =$

8) $\dfrac{1}{12} + \dfrac{4}{12} =$

9) $\dfrac{1}{4} + \dfrac{1}{4} =$

10) $\dfrac{2}{9} + \dfrac{6}{9} =$

Find the sum.

1) $\dfrac{1}{12} + \dfrac{2}{12} =$

2) $\dfrac{4}{9} + \dfrac{4}{9} =$

3) $\dfrac{2}{11} + \dfrac{3}{11} =$

4) $\dfrac{2}{7} + \dfrac{4}{7} =$

5) $\dfrac{1}{10} + \dfrac{6}{10} =$

6) $\dfrac{1}{8} + \dfrac{4}{8} =$

7) $\dfrac{1}{12} + \dfrac{4}{12} =$

8) $\dfrac{1}{6} + \dfrac{2}{6} =$

9) $\dfrac{3}{10} + \dfrac{6}{10} =$

10) $\dfrac{1}{3} + \dfrac{1}{3} =$

Find the sum. Show the solution on the space provided.

1) $\dfrac{6}{7} + \dfrac{8}{28} = \dfrac{24}{28} + \dfrac{8}{28} = \dfrac{32}{28} = \dfrac{8}{7} = 1\dfrac{1}{7}$

2) $\dfrac{3}{7} + \dfrac{3}{21} =$

3) $\dfrac{11}{13} + \dfrac{5}{26} =$

4) $\dfrac{5}{10} + \dfrac{2}{30} =$

5) $\dfrac{8}{26} + \dfrac{9}{13} =$

6) $\dfrac{3}{14} + \dfrac{2}{7} =$

7) $\dfrac{2}{4} + \dfrac{4}{8} =$

8) $\dfrac{9}{20} + \dfrac{1}{5} =$

9) $\dfrac{2}{28} + \dfrac{6}{7} =$

10) $\dfrac{3}{7} + \dfrac{8}{21} =$

Find the sum. Show the solution on the space provided.

1) $\dfrac{5}{6} + \dfrac{4}{12} =$

2) $\dfrac{3}{4} + \dfrac{2}{7} =$

3) $\dfrac{6}{22} + \dfrac{2}{11} =$

4) $\dfrac{1}{7} + \dfrac{9}{14} =$

5) $\dfrac{1}{10} + \dfrac{4}{5} =$

6) $\dfrac{5}{9} + \dfrac{2}{6} =$

7) $\dfrac{6}{7} + \dfrac{2}{21} =$

8) $\dfrac{6}{7} + \dfrac{10}{21} =$

9) $\dfrac{7}{12} + \dfrac{11}{24} =$

10) $\dfrac{5}{16} + \dfrac{2}{4} =$

**Find the sum. Show the solution
on the space provided.**

1) $\dfrac{2}{5} + \dfrac{3}{4} =$

2) $\dfrac{3}{7} + \dfrac{3}{21} =$

3) $\dfrac{1}{8} + \dfrac{3}{4} =$

4) $\dfrac{1}{14} + \dfrac{3}{4} =$

5) $\dfrac{1}{3} + \dfrac{4}{12} =$

6) $\dfrac{2}{6} + \dfrac{3}{4} =$

7) $\dfrac{1}{27} + \dfrac{6}{9} =$

8) $\dfrac{5}{16} + \dfrac{1}{4} =$

9) $\dfrac{3}{7} + \dfrac{6}{21} =$

10) $\dfrac{4}{9} + \dfrac{9}{18} =$

Find the sum. Show the solution on the space provided.

1) $\dfrac{2}{27} + \dfrac{3}{9} =$

2) $\dfrac{1}{6} + \dfrac{8}{9} =$

3) $\dfrac{11}{13} + \dfrac{2}{26} =$

4) $\dfrac{3}{30} + \dfrac{3}{5} =$

5) $\dfrac{9}{28} + \dfrac{3}{7} =$

6) $\dfrac{3}{27} + \dfrac{6}{9} =$

7) $\dfrac{1}{9} + \dfrac{2}{6} =$

8) $\dfrac{2}{10} + \dfrac{2}{4} =$

9) $\dfrac{3}{7} + \dfrac{9}{28} =$

10) $\dfrac{10}{14} + \dfrac{4}{7} =$

Find the sum. Show the solution on the space provided.

1) $\dfrac{1}{3} + \dfrac{4}{6} =$

2) $\dfrac{6}{15} + \dfrac{1}{3} =$

3) $\dfrac{12}{27} + \dfrac{7}{9} =$

4) $\dfrac{6}{20} + \dfrac{3}{4} =$

5) $\dfrac{1}{7} + \dfrac{4}{21} =$

6) $\dfrac{3}{4} + \dfrac{5}{16} =$

7) $\dfrac{11}{27} + \dfrac{5}{9} =$

8) $\dfrac{1}{4} + \dfrac{3}{14} =$

9) $\dfrac{2}{30} + \dfrac{2}{3} =$

10) $\dfrac{3}{4} + \dfrac{3}{12} =$

Find the sum. Show the solution on the space provided.

1) $\dfrac{1}{3} + \dfrac{3}{9} =$

2) $\dfrac{3}{9} + \dfrac{1}{18} =$

3) $\dfrac{2}{12} + \dfrac{2}{6} =$

4) $\dfrac{2}{9} + \dfrac{9}{27} =$

5) $\dfrac{1}{9} + \dfrac{6}{27} =$

6) $\dfrac{9}{14} + \dfrac{6}{7} =$

7) $\dfrac{12}{14} + \dfrac{1}{7} =$

8) $\dfrac{1}{4} + \dfrac{2}{12} =$

9) $\dfrac{2}{3} + \dfrac{4}{15} =$

10) $\dfrac{5}{22} + \dfrac{2}{11} =$

Find the sum. Show the solution on the space provided.

1) $\dfrac{2}{3} + \dfrac{1}{2} =$

2) $\dfrac{1}{2} + \dfrac{3}{10} =$

3) $\dfrac{1}{5} + \dfrac{2}{3} =$

4) $\dfrac{2}{4} + \dfrac{2}{3} =$

5) $\dfrac{1}{2} + \dfrac{2}{5} =$

6) $\dfrac{4}{10} + \dfrac{2}{3} =$

7) $\dfrac{2}{10} + \dfrac{2}{3} =$

8) $\dfrac{3}{4} + \dfrac{1}{5} =$

9) $\dfrac{1}{2} + \dfrac{1}{4} =$

10) $\dfrac{2}{10} + \dfrac{2}{3} =$

Find the sum. Show the solution on the space provided.

1) $1\frac{1}{3} + 4\frac{7}{10} =$

2) $3\frac{2}{3} + 5\frac{2}{5} =$

3) $1\frac{1}{5} + 7\frac{1}{2} =$

4) $1\frac{2}{5} + 9\frac{1}{3} =$

5) $5\frac{1}{2} + 6\frac{4}{5} =$

6) $4\frac{1}{3} + 6\frac{4}{5} =$

7) $2\frac{4}{10} + 7\frac{1}{5} =$

8) $2\frac{5}{10} + 8\frac{1}{2} =$

9) $2\frac{2}{3} + 8\frac{2}{5} =$

10) $5\frac{4}{5} + 4\frac{1}{2} =$

Find the sum. Show the solution on the space provided.

1) $2\frac{3}{5} + 4\frac{2}{4} =$

2) $6\frac{2}{4} + 5\frac{1}{2} =$

3) $2\frac{1}{4} + 4\frac{2}{3} =$

4) $1\frac{1}{2} + 4\frac{2}{4} =$

5) $1\frac{1}{3} + 9\frac{3}{4} =$

6) $5\frac{1}{4} + 9\frac{1}{5} =$

7) $3\frac{7}{10} + 4\frac{3}{4} =$

8) $3\frac{2}{5} + 9\frac{1}{4} =$

9) $5\frac{1}{2} + 6\frac{1}{3} =$

10) $2\frac{2}{3} + 8\frac{1}{2} =$

Find the sum. Show the solution on the space provided.

1) $3\frac{1}{3} + 6\frac{4}{5} =$

2) $1\frac{9}{10} + 8\frac{1}{4} =$

3) $4\frac{1}{2} + 8\frac{4}{5} =$

4) $4\frac{3}{10} + 9\frac{1}{2} =$

5) $4\frac{1}{3} + 4\frac{1}{2} =$

6) $2\frac{3}{5} + 8\frac{4}{10} =$

7) $4\frac{1}{3} + 9\frac{2}{5} =$

8) $6\frac{1}{4} + 5\frac{1}{3} =$

9) $1\frac{2}{3} + 9\frac{1}{2} =$

10) $3\frac{8}{10} + 5\frac{1}{4} =$

**Find the sum. Show the solution
on the space provided.**

1) $5\frac{1}{2} + 7\frac{9}{10} =$

2) $4\frac{3}{4} + 6\frac{2}{5} =$

3) $2\frac{1}{2} + 7\frac{2}{3} =$

4) $2\frac{1}{3} + 9\frac{1}{2} =$

5) $2\frac{6}{10} + 7\frac{1}{4} =$

6) $3\frac{3}{10} + 5\frac{1}{2} =$

7) $3\frac{2}{3} + 8\frac{4}{5} =$

8) $5\frac{1}{4} + 4\frac{4}{5} =$

9) $6\frac{3}{4} + 9\frac{1}{2} =$

10) $2\frac{1}{4} + 5\frac{4}{5} =$

Find the sum. Show the solution on the space provided.

1) $3\frac{2}{3} + 8\frac{9}{10} =$

2) $6\frac{1}{2} + 7\frac{1}{5} =$

3) $2\frac{5}{10} + 6\frac{1}{2} =$

4) $1\frac{3}{10} + 4\frac{2}{5} =$

5) $5\frac{2}{4} + 8\frac{2}{3} =$

6) $6\frac{1}{5} + 8\frac{8}{10} =$

7) $1\frac{1}{3} + 9\frac{1}{4} =$

8) $3\frac{2}{5} + 4\frac{2}{4} =$

9) $6\frac{2}{3} + 7\frac{1}{2} =$

10) $1\frac{4}{5} + 7\frac{1}{4} =$

**Find the sum. Show the solution
on the space provided.**

1) $\quad 1\dfrac{1}{2} + 6\dfrac{2}{5} =$

2) $\quad 1\dfrac{2}{4} + 4\dfrac{1}{3} =$

3) $\quad 4\dfrac{2}{4} + 8\dfrac{1}{5} =$

4) $\quad 4\dfrac{5}{10} + 4\dfrac{2}{4} =$

5) $\quad 6\dfrac{5}{10} + 6\dfrac{1}{2} =$

6) $\quad 6\dfrac{1}{2} + 6\dfrac{2}{3} =$

7) $\quad 6\dfrac{2}{4} + 5\dfrac{1}{5} =$

8) $\quad 4\dfrac{5}{10} + 6\dfrac{2}{3} =$

9) $\quad 4\dfrac{3}{5} + 4\dfrac{4}{10} =$

10) $\quad 4\dfrac{2}{10} + 6\dfrac{3}{4} =$

Find the difference and shade the figure with the indicated fraction.

1)

$$\frac{8}{8} - \frac{7}{8} = \frac{1}{8}$$

2)

$$\frac{8}{8} - \frac{6}{8} = \underline{\hspace{1cm}}$$

3)

$$\frac{6}{8} - \frac{4}{8} = \underline{\hspace{1cm}}$$

4)

$$\frac{5}{9} - \frac{4}{9} = \underline{\hspace{1cm}}$$

5)

$$\frac{7}{9} - \frac{2}{9} = \underline{\hspace{1cm}}$$

Find the difference and shade the figure with the indicated fraction.

EXERCISE 25

1)

$\dfrac{7}{7} - \dfrac{3}{7} =$ _____

2)

$\dfrac{3}{7} - \dfrac{2}{7} =$ _____

3)

$\dfrac{9}{12} - \dfrac{3}{12} =$ _____

4)

$\dfrac{8}{10} - \dfrac{7}{10} =$ _____

5)

$\dfrac{4}{12} - \dfrac{3}{12} =$ _____

Find the difference and shade the figure with the indicated fraction.

1)

$$\frac{8}{10} - \frac{4}{10} = \underline{\hspace{2cm}}$$

2)

$$\frac{3}{11} - \frac{2}{11} = \underline{\hspace{2cm}}$$

3)

$$\frac{7}{8} - \frac{4}{8} = \underline{\hspace{2cm}}$$

4)

$$\frac{6}{6} - \frac{1}{6} = \underline{\hspace{2cm}}$$

5)

$$\frac{5}{9} - \frac{3}{9} = \underline{\hspace{2cm}}$$

		EXERCISE
Find the difference and shade the figure with the indicated fraction.		**27**

1)

$$\frac{2}{5} - \frac{1}{5} = \underline{\quad}$$

2)

$$\frac{5}{6} - \frac{2}{6} = \underline{\quad}$$

3)

$$\frac{8}{11} - \frac{4}{11} = \underline{\quad}$$

4)

$$\frac{2}{3} - \frac{1}{3} = \underline{\quad}$$

5)

$$\frac{9}{10} - \frac{1}{10} = \underline{\quad}$$

Find the difference and shade the figure with the indicated fraction.

1)

$$\frac{3}{7} - \frac{2}{7} = \underline{\hspace{1cm}}$$

2)

$$\frac{9}{12} - \frac{4}{12} = \underline{\hspace{1cm}}$$

3)

$$\frac{9}{10} - \frac{8}{10} = \underline{\hspace{1cm}}$$

4)

$$\frac{4}{11} - \frac{2}{11} = \underline{\hspace{1cm}}$$

5)

$$\frac{11}{11} - \frac{9}{11} = \underline{\hspace{1cm}}$$

Find the difference.

1) $\dfrac{3}{8} - \dfrac{2}{8} = \quad \dfrac{1}{8}$

2) $\dfrac{8}{10} - \dfrac{5}{10} =$

3) $\dfrac{3}{6} - \dfrac{2}{6} =$

4) $\dfrac{3}{11} - \dfrac{1}{11} =$

5) $\dfrac{2}{4} - \dfrac{1}{4} =$

6) $\dfrac{4}{9} - \dfrac{2}{9} =$

7) $\dfrac{3}{9} - \dfrac{2}{9} =$

8) $\dfrac{2}{12} - \dfrac{1}{12} =$

9) $\dfrac{2}{10} - \dfrac{1}{10} =$

10) $\dfrac{5}{12} - \dfrac{1}{12} =$

Find the difference.

1) $\dfrac{9}{11} - \dfrac{6}{11} =$

2) $\dfrac{2}{12} - \dfrac{1}{12} =$

3) $\dfrac{2}{3} - \dfrac{1}{3} =$

4) $\dfrac{10}{11} - \dfrac{8}{11} =$

5) $\dfrac{5}{9} - \dfrac{1}{9} =$

6) $\dfrac{3}{4} - \dfrac{2}{4} =$

7) $\dfrac{2}{10} - \dfrac{1}{10} =$

8) $\dfrac{4}{7} - \dfrac{2}{7} =$

9) $\dfrac{2}{5} - \dfrac{1}{5} =$

10) $\dfrac{4}{12} - \dfrac{3}{12} =$

Find the difference.

1) $\dfrac{9}{12} - \dfrac{3}{12} =$

2) $\dfrac{3}{10} - \dfrac{1}{10} =$

3) $\dfrac{2}{10} - \dfrac{1}{10} =$

4) $\dfrac{8}{9} - \dfrac{5}{9} =$

5) $\dfrac{2}{3} - \dfrac{1}{3} =$

6) $\dfrac{9}{12} - \dfrac{7}{12} =$

7) $\dfrac{5}{9} - \dfrac{2}{9} =$

8) $\dfrac{2}{6} - \dfrac{1}{6} =$

9) $\dfrac{2}{5} - \dfrac{1}{5} =$

10) $\dfrac{3}{4} - \dfrac{1}{4} =$

Find the difference.

1) $\dfrac{2}{5} - \dfrac{1}{5} =$

2) $\dfrac{6}{11} - \dfrac{5}{11} =$

3) $\dfrac{4}{12} - \dfrac{1}{12} =$

4) $\dfrac{9}{12} - \dfrac{2}{12} =$

5) $\dfrac{7}{10} - \dfrac{5}{10} =$

6) $\dfrac{6}{9} - \dfrac{5}{9} =$

7) $\dfrac{2}{3} - \dfrac{1}{3} =$

8) $\dfrac{3}{12} - \dfrac{2}{12} =$

9) $\dfrac{2}{4} - \dfrac{1}{4} =$

10) $\dfrac{4}{10} - \dfrac{2}{10} =$

Find the difference.

1) $\dfrac{3}{4} - \dfrac{2}{4} =$

2) $\dfrac{9}{12} - \dfrac{8}{12} =$

3) $\dfrac{2}{6} - \dfrac{1}{6} =$

4) $\dfrac{4}{5} - \dfrac{2}{5} =$

5) $\dfrac{8}{9} - \dfrac{5}{9} =$

6) $\dfrac{2}{3} - \dfrac{1}{3} =$

7) $\dfrac{2}{11} - \dfrac{1}{11} =$

8) $\dfrac{3}{8} - \dfrac{2}{8} =$

9) $\dfrac{5}{7} - \dfrac{1}{7} =$

10) $\dfrac{8}{12} - \dfrac{1}{12} =$

Find the difference. Show the solution on the space provided.

1) $\dfrac{8}{10} - \dfrac{1}{4} = \dfrac{16}{20} - \dfrac{5}{20} = \dfrac{11}{20}$

2) $\dfrac{6}{10} - \dfrac{1}{2} =$

3) $\dfrac{4}{5} - \dfrac{1}{2} =$

4) $\dfrac{2}{4} - \dfrac{1}{5} =$

5) $\dfrac{7}{10} - \dfrac{1}{3} =$

6) $\dfrac{1}{3} - \dfrac{1}{4} =$

7) $\dfrac{7}{10} - \dfrac{1}{2} =$

8) $\dfrac{1}{2} - \dfrac{1}{3} =$

9) $\dfrac{3}{4} - \dfrac{1}{2} =$

10) $\dfrac{1}{2} - \dfrac{1}{3} =$

Find the difference. Show the solution on the space provided.

EXERCISE
35

1) $\dfrac{3}{4} - \dfrac{2}{3} =$

2) $\dfrac{2}{4} - \dfrac{4}{10} =$

3) $\dfrac{3}{4} - \dfrac{1}{2} =$

4) $\dfrac{1}{2} - \dfrac{1}{3} =$

5) $\dfrac{1}{4} - \dfrac{1}{5} =$

6) $\dfrac{6}{10} - \dfrac{2}{5} =$

7) $\dfrac{1}{2} - \dfrac{1}{4} =$

8) $\dfrac{1}{2} - \dfrac{1}{3} =$

9) $\dfrac{2}{3} - \dfrac{1}{2} =$

10) $\dfrac{3}{10} - \dfrac{1}{5} =$

Find the difference. Show the solution on the space provided.	**EXERCISE 36**

1) $\dfrac{3}{5}$ - $\dfrac{1}{4}$ =

2) $\dfrac{2}{3}$ - $\dfrac{1}{2}$ =

3) $\dfrac{1}{2}$ - $\dfrac{2}{5}$ =

4) $\dfrac{1}{2}$ - $\dfrac{2}{5}$ =

5) $\dfrac{3}{5}$ - $\dfrac{1}{2}$ =

6) $\dfrac{1}{4}$ - $\dfrac{1}{5}$ =

7) $\dfrac{2}{3}$ - $\dfrac{2}{5}$ =

8) $\dfrac{9}{10}$ - $\dfrac{2}{5}$ =

9) $\dfrac{2}{3}$ - $\dfrac{1}{2}$ =

10) $\dfrac{2}{3}$ - $\dfrac{2}{4}$ =

Find the difference. Show the solution on the space provided.

EXERCISE
37

1) $\dfrac{2}{3} - \dfrac{1}{5} =$

2) $\dfrac{1}{3} - \dfrac{1}{4} =$

3) $\dfrac{2}{5} - \dfrac{1}{3} =$

4) $\dfrac{3}{4} - \dfrac{1}{10} =$

5) $\dfrac{1}{5} - \dfrac{1}{10} =$

6) $\dfrac{3}{5} - \dfrac{5}{10} =$

7) $\dfrac{1}{2} - \dfrac{1}{3} =$

8) $\dfrac{9}{10} - \dfrac{1}{2} =$

9) $\dfrac{2}{3} - \dfrac{1}{10} =$

10) $\dfrac{8}{10} - \dfrac{1}{4} =$

Find the difference. Show the solution on the space provided.

1) $\dfrac{6}{8} - \dfrac{8}{16} =$

2) $\dfrac{8}{12} - \dfrac{1}{8} =$

3) $\dfrac{8}{14} - \dfrac{2}{7} =$

4) $\dfrac{10}{30} - \dfrac{1}{3} =$

5) $\dfrac{4}{6} - \dfrac{4}{8} =$

6) $\dfrac{4}{7} - \dfrac{9}{21} =$

7) $\dfrac{5}{9} - \dfrac{1}{3} =$

8) $\dfrac{2}{3} - \dfrac{5}{18} =$

9) $\dfrac{7}{15} - \dfrac{2}{6} =$

10) $\dfrac{8}{28} - \dfrac{1}{14} =$

Find the difference. Show the solution on the space provided.

EXERCISE

39

1) $\dfrac{4}{16} - \dfrac{1}{8} =$

2) $\dfrac{12}{16} - \dfrac{5}{8} =$

3) $\dfrac{3}{4} - \dfrac{5}{24} =$

4) $\dfrac{7}{11} - \dfrac{10}{22} =$

5) $\dfrac{2}{6} - \dfrac{3}{18} =$

6) $\dfrac{5}{7} - \dfrac{10}{28} =$

7) $\dfrac{4}{11} - \dfrac{7}{22} =$

8) $\dfrac{12}{14} - \dfrac{1}{28} =$

9) $\dfrac{2}{3} - \dfrac{6}{18} =$

10) $\dfrac{1}{9} - \dfrac{1}{27} =$

Find the difference. Show the solution on the space provided.

1) $\dfrac{3}{4} - \dfrac{4}{14} =$

2) $\dfrac{2}{6} - \dfrac{3}{15} =$

3) $\dfrac{5}{13} - \dfrac{9}{26} =$

4) $\dfrac{3}{5} - \dfrac{4}{30} =$

5) $\dfrac{5}{12} - \dfrac{1}{4} =$

6) $\dfrac{6}{14} - \dfrac{3}{7} =$

7) $\dfrac{6}{7} - \dfrac{5}{21} =$

8) $\dfrac{4}{6} - \dfrac{11}{24} =$

9) $\dfrac{8}{14} - \dfrac{1}{28} =$

10) $\dfrac{4}{11} - \dfrac{3}{22} =$

Find the difference. Show the solution on the space provided.

1) $9\frac{1}{3} - 2\frac{1}{4} =$

2) $8\frac{1}{3} - 3\frac{1}{5} =$

3) $8\frac{1}{2} - 2\frac{3}{10} =$

4) $5\frac{2}{4} - 3\frac{2}{10} =$

5) $9\frac{2}{5} - 1\frac{3}{10} =$

6) $5\frac{1}{2} - 2\frac{2}{10} =$

7) $9\frac{4}{5} - 2\frac{1}{3} =$

8) $6\frac{3}{4} - 2\frac{3}{5} =$

9) $9\frac{9}{10} - 3\frac{1}{3} =$

10) $7\frac{3}{4} - 3\frac{1}{5} =$

Find the difference. Show the solution on the space provided.

1) $7\frac{8}{10} - 3\frac{1}{3} =$

2) $8\frac{4}{5} - 1\frac{1}{3} =$

3) $8\frac{2}{3} - 4\frac{1}{5} =$

4) $8\frac{1}{2} - 3\frac{1}{10} =$

5) $6\frac{1}{2} - 2\frac{2}{5} =$

6) $9\frac{3}{5} - 4\frac{6}{10} =$

7) $7\frac{2}{3} - 2\frac{1}{4} =$

8) $7\frac{2}{4} - 1\frac{1}{3} =$

9) $5\frac{1}{3} - 2\frac{3}{10} =$

10) $9\frac{1}{2} - 3\frac{1}{4} =$

Find the difference. Show the solution on the space provided.

1) $6\frac{2}{4} - 1\frac{1}{2} =$

2) $6\frac{1}{3} - 2\frac{1}{5} =$

3) $7\frac{4}{5} - 4\frac{3}{10} =$

4) $6\frac{3}{5} - 4\frac{1}{3} =$

5) $5\frac{3}{4} - 1\frac{1}{5} =$

6) $7\frac{1}{2} - 2\frac{2}{10} =$

7) $8\frac{3}{4} - 1\frac{2}{3} =$

8) $7\frac{3}{4} - 1\frac{2}{3} =$

9) $8\frac{3}{4} - 2\frac{1}{2} =$

10) $8\frac{3}{4} - 3\frac{1}{2} =$

Find the difference. Show the solution on the space provided.

1) $9\frac{1}{2} - 3\frac{1}{3} =$

2) $8\frac{8}{10} - 1\frac{2}{3} =$

3) $5\frac{2}{3} - 3\frac{1}{5} =$

4) $8\frac{3}{4} - 1\frac{1}{10} =$

5) $7\frac{2}{4} - 2\frac{2}{5} =$

6) $5\frac{3}{4} - 3\frac{1}{2} =$

7) $7\frac{1}{2} - 4\frac{2}{10} =$

8) $6\frac{4}{5} - 4\frac{2}{3} =$

9) $7\frac{9}{10} - 2\frac{1}{2} =$

10) $5\frac{4}{5} - 1\frac{2}{3} =$

Find the difference. Show the solution on the space provided.

1) $6\frac{1}{4} - 1\frac{1}{5} =$

2) $8\frac{2}{3} - 3\frac{2}{4} =$

3) $6\frac{3}{4} - 3\frac{7}{10} =$

4) $6\frac{2}{3} - 1\frac{1}{5} =$

5) $6\frac{2}{4} - 2\frac{1}{5} =$

6) $9\frac{2}{5} - 4\frac{1}{3} =$

7) $9\frac{2}{3} - 3\frac{1}{5} =$

8) $8\frac{1}{2} - 2\frac{1}{4} =$

9) $5\frac{1}{4} - 3\frac{1}{10} =$

10) $5\frac{3}{4} - 2\frac{1}{2} =$

Find the difference. Show the solution on the space provided.

1) $7\frac{3}{4} - 4\frac{2}{5} =$

2) $7\frac{3}{4} - 1\frac{1}{2} =$

3) $6\frac{1}{2} - 4\frac{1}{10} =$

4) $6\frac{3}{4} - 3\frac{2}{3} =$

5) $8\frac{1}{3} - 3\frac{1}{4} =$

6) $7\frac{1}{2} - 3\frac{2}{5} =$

7) $9\frac{1}{2} - 4\frac{1}{3} =$

8) $9\frac{2}{3} - 3\frac{1}{5} =$

9) $9\frac{4}{5} - 3\frac{2}{4} =$

10) $6\frac{1}{2} - 3\frac{1}{3} =$

ANSWERS!

EXERCISE 1		EXERCISE 2	

EXERCISE 1

1) $\dfrac{1}{9} + \dfrac{1}{9} = \dfrac{2}{9}$

2) $\dfrac{1}{10} + \dfrac{5}{10} = \dfrac{6}{10}$

3) $\dfrac{1}{5} + \dfrac{3}{5} = \dfrac{4}{5}$

4) $\dfrac{1}{6} + \dfrac{2}{6} = \dfrac{3}{6}$

5) $\dfrac{1}{8} + \dfrac{5}{8} = \dfrac{6}{8}$

EXERCISE 2

1) $\dfrac{3}{12} + \dfrac{8}{12} = \dfrac{11}{12}$

2) $\dfrac{1}{7} + \dfrac{4}{7} = \dfrac{5}{7}$

3) $\dfrac{1}{8} + \dfrac{5}{8} = \dfrac{6}{8}$

4) $\dfrac{2}{6} + \dfrac{2}{6} = \dfrac{4}{6}$

5) $\dfrac{1}{11} + \dfrac{6}{11} = \dfrac{7}{11}$

EXERCISE 3

1)

$$\frac{2}{11} + \frac{7}{11} = \frac{9}{11}$$

2)

$$\frac{1}{3} + \frac{1}{3} = \frac{2}{3}$$

3)

$$\frac{2}{12} + \frac{6}{12} = \frac{8}{12}$$

4)

$$\frac{4}{11} + \frac{6}{11} = \frac{10}{11}$$

5)

$$\frac{1}{10} + \frac{1}{10} = \frac{2}{10}$$

EXERCISE 4

1)

$$\frac{3}{11} + \frac{5}{11} = \frac{8}{11}$$

2)

$$\frac{2}{6} + \frac{3}{6} = \frac{5}{6}$$

3)

$$\frac{1}{11} + \frac{4}{11} = \frac{5}{11}$$

4)

$$\frac{1}{9} + \frac{5}{9} = \frac{6}{9}$$

5)

$$\frac{3}{7} + \frac{3}{7} = \frac{6}{7}$$

EXERCISE 5

1)

$$\frac{2}{10} + \frac{2}{10} = \frac{4}{10}$$

2)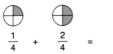

$$\frac{1}{4} + \frac{2}{4} = \frac{3}{4}$$

3)

$$\frac{1}{3} + \frac{1}{3} = \frac{2}{3}$$

4)

$$\frac{2}{12} + \frac{4}{12} = \frac{6}{12}$$

5)

$$\frac{2}{9} + \frac{2}{9} = \frac{4}{9}$$

EXERCISE 6

1) $\frac{1}{10} + \frac{6}{10} = \frac{7}{10}$

2) $\frac{2}{7} + \frac{2}{7} = \frac{4}{7}$

3) $\frac{2}{11} + \frac{4}{11} = \frac{6}{11}$

4) $\frac{1}{5} + \frac{3}{5} = \frac{4}{5}$

5) $\frac{2}{12} + \frac{8}{12} = \frac{10}{12}$

6) $\frac{1}{4} + \frac{2}{4} = \frac{3}{4}$

7) $\frac{4}{12} + \frac{6}{12} = \frac{10}{12}$

8) $\frac{3}{10} + \frac{3}{10} = \frac{6}{10}$

9) $\frac{1}{9} + \frac{4}{9} = \frac{5}{9}$

10) $\frac{1}{6} + \frac{3}{6} = \frac{4}{6}$

EXERCISE 7

1) $\frac{2}{12} + \frac{5}{12} = \frac{7}{12}$

2) $\frac{1}{10} + \frac{6}{10} = \frac{7}{10}$

3) $\frac{3}{10} + \frac{6}{10} = \frac{9}{10}$

4) $\frac{3}{12} + \frac{5}{12} = \frac{8}{12}$

5) $\frac{1}{4} + \frac{1}{4} = \frac{2}{4}$

6) $\frac{1}{5} + \frac{1}{5} = \frac{2}{5}$

7) $\frac{4}{11} + \frac{5}{11} = \frac{9}{11}$

8) $\frac{1}{7} + \frac{3}{7} = \frac{4}{7}$

9) $\frac{1}{9} + \frac{2}{9} = \frac{3}{9}$

10) $\frac{1}{3} + \frac{1}{3} = \frac{2}{3}$

EXERCISE 8

1) $\frac{1}{11} + \frac{2}{11} = \frac{3}{11}$

2) $\frac{1}{9} + \frac{6}{9} = \frac{7}{9}$

3) $\frac{1}{7} + \frac{2}{7} = \frac{3}{7}$

4) $\frac{1}{3} + \frac{1}{3} = \frac{2}{3}$

5) $\frac{2}{12} + \frac{4}{12} = \frac{6}{12}$

6) $\frac{4}{12} + \frac{7}{12} = \frac{11}{12}$

7) $\frac{1}{8} + \frac{6}{8} = \frac{7}{8}$

8) $\frac{1}{5} + \frac{2}{5} = \frac{3}{5}$

9) $\frac{1}{10} + \frac{2}{10} = \frac{3}{10}$

10) $\frac{1}{6} + \frac{3}{6} = \frac{4}{6}$

EXERCISE 9

1) $\frac{3}{12} + \frac{8}{12} = \frac{11}{12}$

2) $\frac{1}{3} + \frac{1}{3} = \frac{2}{3}$

3) $\frac{2}{8} + \frac{3}{8} = \frac{5}{8}$

4) $\frac{1}{6} + \frac{3}{6} = \frac{4}{6}$

5) $\frac{2}{5} + \frac{2}{5} = \frac{4}{5}$

6) $\frac{1}{7} + \frac{5}{7} = \frac{6}{7}$

7) $\frac{1}{11} + \frac{3}{11} = \frac{4}{11}$

8) $\frac{1}{12} + \frac{4}{12} = \frac{5}{12}$

9) $\frac{1}{4} + \frac{1}{4} = \frac{2}{4}$

10) $\frac{2}{9} + \frac{6}{9} = \frac{8}{9}$

EXERCISE 10

1) $\frac{1}{12} + \frac{2}{12} = \frac{3}{12}$

2) $\frac{4}{9} + \frac{4}{9} = \frac{8}{9}$

3) $\frac{2}{11} + \frac{3}{11} = \frac{5}{11}$

4) $\frac{2}{7} + \frac{4}{7} = \frac{6}{7}$

5) $\frac{1}{10} + \frac{6}{10} = \frac{7}{10}$

6) $\frac{1}{8} + \frac{4}{8} = \frac{5}{8}$

7) $\frac{1}{12} + \frac{4}{12} = \frac{5}{12}$

8) $\frac{1}{6} + \frac{2}{6} = \frac{3}{6}$

9) $\frac{3}{10} + \frac{6}{10} = \frac{9}{10}$

10) $\frac{1}{3} + \frac{1}{3} = \frac{2}{3}$

EXERCISE 11

1) $\frac{6}{7} + \frac{8}{28} = \frac{24}{28} + \frac{8}{28} = \frac{32}{28} = \frac{8}{7} = 1\frac{1}{7}$

2) $\frac{3}{7} + \frac{3}{21} = \frac{9}{21} + \frac{3}{21} = \frac{12}{21} = \frac{4}{7}$

3) $\frac{11}{13} + \frac{5}{26} = \frac{22}{26} + \frac{5}{26} = \frac{27}{26} = 1\frac{1}{26}$

4) $\frac{5}{10} + \frac{2}{30} = \frac{15}{30} + \frac{2}{30} = \frac{17}{30}$

5) $\frac{8}{26} + \frac{9}{13} = \frac{8}{26} + \frac{18}{26} = \frac{26}{26} = 1$

6) $\frac{3}{14} + \frac{2}{7} = \frac{3}{14} + \frac{4}{14} = \frac{7}{14} = \frac{1}{2}$

7) $\frac{2}{4} + \frac{4}{8} = \frac{4}{8} + \frac{4}{8} = \frac{8}{8} = 1$

8) $\frac{9}{20} + \frac{1}{5} = \frac{9}{20} + \frac{4}{20} = \frac{13}{20}$

9) $\frac{2}{28} + \frac{6}{7} = \frac{2}{28} + \frac{24}{28} = \frac{26}{28} = \frac{13}{14}$

10) $\frac{3}{7} + \frac{8}{21} = \frac{9}{21} + \frac{8}{21} = \frac{17}{21}$

EXERCISE 12

1) $\frac{5}{6} + \frac{4}{12} = \frac{10}{12} + \frac{4}{12} = \frac{14}{12} = \frac{7}{6} = 1\frac{1}{6}$

2) $\frac{3}{4} + \frac{2}{7} = \frac{21}{28} + \frac{8}{28} = \frac{29}{28} = 1\frac{1}{28}$

3) $\frac{6}{22} + \frac{2}{11} = \frac{6}{22} + \frac{4}{22} = \frac{10}{22} = \frac{5}{11}$

4) $\frac{1}{7} + \frac{9}{14} = \frac{2}{14} + \frac{9}{14} = \frac{11}{14}$

5) $\frac{1}{10} + \frac{4}{5} = \frac{1}{10} + \frac{8}{10} = \frac{9}{10}$

6) $\frac{5}{9} + \frac{2}{6} = \frac{10}{18} + \frac{6}{18} = \frac{16}{18} = \frac{8}{9}$

7) $\frac{6}{7} + \frac{2}{21} = \frac{18}{21} + \frac{2}{21} = \frac{20}{21}$

8) $\frac{6}{7} + \frac{10}{21} = \frac{18}{21} + \frac{10}{21} = \frac{28}{21} = \frac{4}{3} = 1\frac{1}{3}$

9) $\frac{7}{12} + \frac{11}{24} = \frac{14}{24} + \frac{11}{24} = \frac{25}{24} = 1\frac{1}{24}$

10) $\frac{5}{16} + \frac{2}{4} = \frac{5}{16} + \frac{8}{16} = \frac{13}{16}$

EXERCISE 13

1) $\frac{2}{5} + \frac{3}{4} = \frac{8}{20} + \frac{15}{20} = \frac{23}{20} = 1\frac{3}{20}$

2) $\frac{3}{7} + \frac{3}{21} = \frac{9}{21} + \frac{3}{21} = \frac{12}{21} = \frac{4}{7}$

3) $\frac{1}{8} + \frac{3}{4} = \frac{1}{8} + \frac{6}{8} = \frac{7}{8}$

4) $\frac{1}{14} + \frac{3}{4} = \frac{2}{28} + \frac{21}{28} = \frac{23}{28}$

5) $\frac{1}{3} + \frac{4}{12} = \frac{4}{12} + \frac{4}{12} = \frac{8}{12} = \frac{2}{3}$

6) $\frac{2}{6} + \frac{3}{4} = \frac{4}{12} + \frac{9}{12} = \frac{13}{12} = 1\frac{1}{12}$

7) $\frac{1}{27} + \frac{6}{9} = \frac{1}{27} + \frac{18}{27} = \frac{19}{27}$

8) $\frac{5}{16} + \frac{1}{4} = \frac{5}{16} + \frac{4}{16} = \frac{9}{16}$

9) $\frac{3}{7} + \frac{6}{21} = \frac{9}{21} + \frac{6}{21} = \frac{15}{21} = \frac{5}{7}$

10) $\frac{4}{9} + \frac{9}{18} = \frac{8}{18} + \frac{9}{18} = \frac{17}{18}$

EXERCISE 14

1) $\frac{2}{27} + \frac{3}{9} = \frac{2}{27} + \frac{9}{27} = \frac{11}{27}$

2) $\frac{1}{6} + \frac{8}{9} = \frac{3}{18} + \frac{16}{18} = \frac{19}{18} = 1\frac{1}{18}$

3) $\frac{11}{13} + \frac{2}{26} = \frac{22}{26} + \frac{2}{26} = \frac{24}{26} = \frac{12}{13}$

4) $\frac{3}{30} + \frac{3}{5} = \frac{3}{30} + \frac{18}{30} = \frac{21}{30} = \frac{7}{10}$

5) $\frac{9}{28} + \frac{3}{7} = \frac{9}{28} + \frac{12}{28} = \frac{21}{28} = \frac{3}{4}$

6) $\frac{3}{27} + \frac{6}{9} = \frac{3}{27} + \frac{18}{27} = \frac{21}{27} = \frac{7}{9}$

7) $\frac{1}{9} + \frac{2}{6} = \frac{2}{18} + \frac{6}{18} = \frac{8}{18} = \frac{4}{9}$

8) $\frac{2}{10} + \frac{2}{4} = \frac{4}{20} + \frac{10}{20} = \frac{14}{20} = \frac{7}{10}$

9) $\frac{3}{7} + \frac{9}{28} = \frac{12}{28} + \frac{9}{28} = \frac{21}{28} = \frac{3}{4}$

10) $\frac{10}{14} + \frac{4}{7} = \frac{10}{14} + \frac{8}{14} = \frac{18}{14} = \frac{9}{7} = 1\frac{2}{7}$

EXERCISE 15

1) $\frac{1}{3} + \frac{4}{6} =$ $\frac{2}{6} + \frac{4}{6} =$ $\frac{6}{6} =$ 1

2) $\frac{6}{15} + \frac{1}{3} =$ $\frac{6}{15} + \frac{5}{15} =$ $\frac{11}{15}$

3) $\frac{12}{27} + \frac{7}{9} =$ $\frac{12}{27} + \frac{21}{27} =$ $\frac{33}{27} =$ $\frac{11}{9} =$ $1\frac{2}{9}$

4) $\frac{6}{20} + \frac{3}{4} =$ $\frac{6}{20} + \frac{15}{20} =$ $\frac{21}{20} =$ $1\frac{1}{20}$

5) $\frac{1}{7} + \frac{4}{21} =$ $\frac{3}{21} + \frac{4}{21} =$ $\frac{7}{21} =$ $\frac{1}{3}$

6) $\frac{3}{4} + \frac{5}{16} =$ $\frac{12}{16} + \frac{5}{16} =$ $\frac{17}{16} =$ $1\frac{1}{16}$

7) $\frac{11}{27} + \frac{5}{9} =$ $\frac{11}{27} + \frac{15}{27} =$ $\frac{26}{27}$

8) $\frac{1}{4} + \frac{3}{14} =$ $\frac{7}{28} + \frac{6}{28} =$ $\frac{13}{28}$

9) $\frac{2}{30} + \frac{2}{3} =$ $\frac{2}{30} + \frac{20}{30} =$ $\frac{22}{30} =$ $\frac{11}{15}$

10) $\frac{3}{4} + \frac{3}{12} =$ $\frac{9}{12} + \frac{3}{12} =$ $\frac{12}{12} =$ 1

EXERCISE 16

1) $\frac{1}{3} + \frac{3}{9} =$ $\frac{3}{9} + \frac{3}{9} =$ $\frac{6}{9} =$ $\frac{2}{3}$

2) $\frac{3}{9} + \frac{1}{18} =$ $\frac{6}{18} + \frac{1}{18} =$ $\frac{7}{18}$

3) $\frac{2}{12} + \frac{2}{6} =$ $\frac{2}{12} + \frac{4}{12} =$ $\frac{6}{12} =$ $\frac{1}{2}$

4) $\frac{2}{9} + \frac{9}{27} =$ $\frac{6}{27} + \frac{9}{27} =$ $\frac{15}{27} =$ $\frac{5}{9}$

5) $\frac{1}{9} + \frac{6}{27} =$ $\frac{3}{27} + \frac{6}{27} =$ $\frac{9}{27} =$ $\frac{1}{3}$

6) $\frac{9}{14} + \frac{6}{7} =$ $\frac{9}{14} + \frac{12}{14} =$ $\frac{21}{14} =$ $\frac{3}{2} =$ $1\frac{1}{2}$

7) $\frac{12}{14} + \frac{1}{7} =$ $\frac{12}{14} + \frac{2}{14} =$ $\frac{14}{14} =$ 1

8) $\frac{1}{4} + \frac{2}{12} =$ $\frac{3}{12} + \frac{2}{12} =$ $\frac{5}{12}$

9) $\frac{2}{3} + \frac{4}{15} =$ $\frac{10}{15} + \frac{4}{15} =$ $\frac{14}{15}$

10) $\frac{5}{22} + \frac{2}{11} =$ $\frac{5}{22} + \frac{4}{22} =$ $\frac{9}{22}$

EXERCISE 17

1) $\frac{2}{3} + \frac{1}{2} =$ $\frac{4}{6} + \frac{3}{6} =$ $\frac{7}{6} =$ $1\frac{1}{6}$

2) $\frac{1}{2} + \frac{3}{10} =$ $\frac{5}{10} + \frac{3}{10} =$ $\frac{8}{10} =$ $\frac{4}{5}$

3) $\frac{1}{5} + \frac{2}{3} =$ $\frac{3}{15} + \frac{10}{15} =$ $\frac{13}{15}$

4) $\frac{2}{4} + \frac{2}{3} =$ $\frac{6}{12} + \frac{8}{12} =$ $\frac{14}{12} =$ $\frac{7}{6} =$ $1\frac{1}{6}$

5) $\frac{1}{2} + \frac{2}{5} =$ $\frac{5}{10} + \frac{4}{10} =$ $\frac{9}{10}$

6) $\frac{4}{10} + \frac{2}{3} =$ $\frac{12}{30} + \frac{20}{30} =$ $\frac{32}{30} =$ $\frac{16}{15} =$ $1\frac{1}{15}$

7) $\frac{2}{10} + \frac{2}{3} =$ $\frac{6}{30} + \frac{20}{30} =$ $\frac{26}{30} =$ $\frac{13}{15}$

8) $\frac{3}{4} + \frac{1}{5} =$ $\frac{15}{20} + \frac{4}{20} =$ $\frac{19}{20}$

9) $\frac{1}{2} + \frac{1}{4} =$ $\frac{2}{4} + \frac{1}{4} =$ $\frac{3}{4}$

10) $\frac{2}{10} + \frac{2}{3} =$ $\frac{6}{30} + \frac{20}{30} =$ $\frac{26}{30} =$ $\frac{13}{15}$

EXERCISE 18

1) $1\frac{1}{3} + 4\frac{7}{10} =$ $1\frac{10}{30} + 4\frac{21}{30} =$ $5\frac{31}{30} =$ $6\frac{1}{30}$

2) $3\frac{2}{3} + 5\frac{2}{5} =$ $3\frac{10}{15} + 5\frac{6}{15} =$ $8\frac{16}{15} =$ $9\frac{1}{15}$

3) $1\frac{1}{5} + 7\frac{1}{2} =$ $1\frac{2}{10} + 7\frac{5}{10} =$ $8\frac{7}{10}$

4) $1\frac{2}{5} + 9\frac{1}{3} =$ $1\frac{6}{15} + 9\frac{5}{15} =$ $10\frac{11}{15}$

5) $5\frac{1}{2} + 6\frac{4}{5} =$ $5\frac{5}{10} + 6\frac{8}{10} =$ $11\frac{13}{10} =$ $12\frac{3}{10}$

6) $4\frac{1}{3} + 6\frac{4}{5} =$ $4\frac{5}{15} + 6\frac{12}{15} =$ $10\frac{17}{15} =$ $11\frac{2}{15}$

7) $2\frac{4}{10} + 7\frac{1}{5} =$ $2\frac{4}{10} + 7\frac{2}{10} =$ $9\frac{6}{10} =$ $9\frac{3}{5}$

8) $2\frac{5}{10} + 8\frac{1}{2} =$ $2\frac{5}{10} + 8\frac{5}{10} =$ $10\frac{10}{10} =$ 11

9) $2\frac{2}{3} + 8\frac{2}{5} =$ $2\frac{10}{15} + 8\frac{6}{15} =$ $10\frac{16}{15} =$ $11\frac{1}{15}$

0) $5\frac{4}{5} + 4\frac{1}{2} =$ $5\frac{8}{10} + 4\frac{5}{10} =$ $9\frac{13}{10} =$ $10\frac{3}{10}$

EXERCISE 19

1) $2\frac{3}{5} + 4\frac{2}{4} =$ $2\frac{12}{20} + 4\frac{10}{20} =$ $6\frac{22}{20} =$ $7\frac{1}{10}$

2) $6\frac{2}{4} + 5\frac{1}{2} =$ $6\frac{2}{4} + 5\frac{2}{4} =$ $11\frac{4}{4} =$ 12

3) $2\frac{1}{4} + 4\frac{2}{3} =$ $2\frac{3}{12} + 4\frac{8}{12} =$ $6\frac{11}{12}$

4) $1\frac{1}{2} + 4\frac{2}{4} =$ $1\frac{2}{4} + 4\frac{2}{4} =$ $5\frac{4}{4} =$ 6

5) $1\frac{1}{3} + 9\frac{3}{4} =$ $1\frac{4}{12} + 9\frac{9}{12} =$ $10\frac{13}{12} =$ $11\frac{1}{12}$

6) $5\frac{1}{4} + 9\frac{1}{5} =$ $5\frac{5}{20} + 9\frac{4}{20} =$ $14\frac{9}{20}$

7) $3\frac{7}{10} + 4\frac{3}{4} =$ $3\frac{14}{20} + 4\frac{15}{20} =$ $7\frac{29}{20} =$ $8\frac{9}{20}$

8) $3\frac{2}{5} + 9\frac{1}{4} =$ $3\frac{8}{20} + 9\frac{5}{20} =$ $12\frac{13}{20}$

9) $5\frac{1}{2} + 6\frac{1}{3} =$ $5\frac{3}{6} + 6\frac{2}{6} =$ $11\frac{5}{6}$

0) $2\frac{2}{3} + 8\frac{1}{2} =$ $2\frac{4}{6} + 8\frac{3}{6} =$ $10\frac{7}{6} =$ $11\frac{1}{6}$

EXERCISE 20

1) $3\frac{1}{3} + 6\frac{4}{5} =$ $3\frac{5}{15} + 6\frac{12}{15} =$ $9\frac{17}{15} =$ $10\frac{2}{15}$

2) $1\frac{9}{10} + 8\frac{1}{4} =$ $1\frac{18}{20} + 8\frac{5}{20} =$ $9\frac{23}{20} =$ $10\frac{3}{20}$

3) $4\frac{1}{2} + 8\frac{4}{5} =$ $4\frac{5}{10} + 8\frac{8}{10} =$ $12\frac{13}{10} =$ $13\frac{3}{10}$

4) $4\frac{3}{10} + 9\frac{1}{2} =$ $4\frac{3}{10} + 9\frac{5}{10} =$ $13\frac{8}{10} =$ $13\frac{4}{5}$

5) $4\frac{1}{3} + 4\frac{1}{2} =$ $4\frac{2}{6} + 4\frac{3}{6} =$ $8\frac{5}{6}$

6) $2\frac{3}{5} + 8\frac{4}{10} =$ $2\frac{6}{10} + 8\frac{4}{10} =$ $10\frac{10}{10} =$ 11

7) $4\frac{1}{3} + 9\frac{2}{5} =$ $4\frac{5}{15} + 9\frac{6}{15} =$ $13\frac{11}{15}$

8) $6\frac{1}{4} + 5\frac{1}{3} =$ $6\frac{3}{12} + 5\frac{4}{12} =$ $11\frac{7}{12}$

9) $1\frac{2}{3} + 9\frac{1}{2} =$ $1\frac{4}{6} + 9\frac{3}{6} =$ $10\frac{7}{6} =$ $11\frac{1}{6}$

0) $3\frac{8}{10} + 5\frac{1}{4} =$ $3\frac{16}{20} + 5\frac{5}{20} =$ $8\frac{21}{20} =$ $9\frac{1}{20}$

EXERCISE 21

1) $5\frac{1}{2} + 7\frac{9}{10} =$ $5\frac{5}{10} + 7\frac{9}{10} =$ $12\frac{14}{10} =$ $13\frac{2}{5}$

2) $4\frac{3}{4} + 6\frac{2}{5} =$ $4\frac{15}{20} + 6\frac{8}{20} =$ $10\frac{23}{20} =$ $11\frac{3}{20}$

3) $2\frac{1}{2} + 7\frac{2}{3} =$ $2\frac{3}{6} + 7\frac{4}{6} =$ $9\frac{7}{6} =$ $10\frac{1}{6}$

4) $2\frac{1}{3} + 9\frac{1}{2} =$ $2\frac{2}{6} + 9\frac{3}{6} =$ $11\frac{5}{6}$

5) $2\frac{6}{10} + 7\frac{1}{4} =$ $2\frac{12}{20} + 7\frac{5}{20} =$ $9\frac{17}{20}$

6) $3\frac{3}{10} + 5\frac{1}{2} =$ $3\frac{3}{10} + 5\frac{5}{10} =$ $8\frac{8}{10} =$ $8\frac{4}{5}$

7) $3\frac{2}{3} + 8\frac{4}{5} =$ $3\frac{10}{15} + 8\frac{12}{15} =$ $11\frac{22}{15} =$ $12\frac{7}{15}$

8) $5\frac{1}{4} + 4\frac{4}{5} =$ $5\frac{5}{20} + 4\frac{16}{20} =$ $9\frac{21}{20} =$ $10\frac{1}{20}$

9) $6\frac{3}{4} + 9\frac{1}{2} =$ $6\frac{3}{4} + 9\frac{2}{4} =$ $15\frac{5}{4} =$ $16\frac{1}{4}$

0) $2\frac{1}{4} + 5\frac{4}{5} =$ $2\frac{5}{20} + 5\frac{16}{20} =$ $7\frac{21}{20} =$ $8\frac{1}{20}$

EXERCISE 22

1) $3\frac{2}{3} + 8\frac{9}{10} =$ $3\frac{20}{30} + 8\frac{27}{30} =$ $11\frac{47}{30} =$ $12\frac{17}{30}$

2) $6\frac{1}{2} + 7\frac{1}{5} =$ $6\frac{5}{10} + 7\frac{2}{10} =$ $13\frac{7}{10}$

3) $2\frac{5}{10} + 6\frac{1}{2} =$ $2\frac{5}{10} + 6\frac{5}{10} =$ $8\frac{10}{10} =$ 9

4) $1\frac{3}{10} + 4\frac{2}{5} =$ $1\frac{3}{10} + 4\frac{4}{10} =$ $5\frac{7}{10}$

5) $5\frac{2}{4} + 8\frac{2}{3} =$ $5\frac{6}{12} + 8\frac{8}{12} =$ $13\frac{14}{12} =$ $14\frac{1}{6}$

6) $6\frac{1}{5} + 8\frac{8}{10} =$ $6\frac{2}{10} + 8\frac{8}{10} =$ $14\frac{10}{10} =$ 15

7) $1\frac{1}{3} + 9\frac{1}{4} =$ $1\frac{4}{12} + 9\frac{3}{12} =$ $10\frac{7}{12}$

8) $3\frac{2}{5} + 4\frac{2}{4} =$ $3\frac{8}{20} + 4\frac{10}{20} =$ $7\frac{18}{20} =$ $7\frac{9}{10}$

9) $6\frac{2}{3} + 7\frac{1}{2} =$ $6\frac{4}{6} + 7\frac{3}{6} =$ $13\frac{7}{6} =$ $14\frac{1}{6}$

0) $1\frac{4}{5} + 7\frac{1}{4} =$ $1\frac{16}{20} + 7\frac{5}{20} =$ $8\frac{21}{20} =$ $9\frac{1}{20}$

EXERCISE 23

1) $1\frac{1}{2} + 6\frac{2}{5} =$ $1\frac{5}{10} + 6\frac{4}{10} =$ $7\frac{9}{10}$

2) $1\frac{2}{4} + 4\frac{1}{3} =$ $1\frac{6}{12} + 4\frac{4}{12} =$ $5\frac{10}{12} =$ $5\frac{5}{6}$

3) $4\frac{2}{4} + 8\frac{1}{5} =$ $4\frac{10}{20} + 8\frac{4}{20} =$ $12\frac{14}{20} =$ $12\frac{7}{10}$

4) $4\frac{5}{10} + 4\frac{2}{4} =$ $4\frac{10}{20} + 4\frac{10}{20} =$ $8\frac{20}{20} =$ 9

5) $6\frac{5}{10} + 6\frac{1}{2} =$ $6\frac{5}{10} + 6\frac{5}{10} =$ $12\frac{10}{10} =$ 13

6) $6\frac{1}{2} + 6\frac{2}{3} =$ $6\frac{3}{6} + 6\frac{4}{6} =$ $12\frac{7}{6} =$ $13\frac{1}{6}$

7) $6\frac{2}{4} + 5\frac{1}{5} =$ $6\frac{10}{20} + 5\frac{4}{20} =$ $11\frac{14}{20} =$ $11\frac{7}{10}$

8) $4\frac{5}{10} + 6\frac{2}{3} =$ $4\frac{15}{30} + 6\frac{20}{30} =$ $10\frac{35}{30} =$ $11\frac{1}{6}$

9) $4\frac{3}{5} + 4\frac{4}{10} =$ $4\frac{6}{10} + 4\frac{4}{10} =$ $8\frac{10}{10} =$ 9

0) $4\frac{2}{10} + 6\frac{3}{4} =$ $4\frac{4}{20} + 6\frac{15}{20} =$ $10\frac{19}{20}$

EXERCISE 24

1) $\frac{8}{8} - \frac{7}{8} = \frac{1}{8}$

2) $\frac{8}{8} - \frac{6}{8} = \frac{2}{8}$

3) $\frac{6}{8} - \frac{4}{8} = \frac{2}{8}$

4) $\frac{5}{9} - \frac{4}{9} = \frac{1}{9}$

5) $\frac{7}{9} - \frac{2}{9} = \frac{5}{9}$

EXERCISE 25

1) $\frac{7}{7} - \frac{3}{7} = \frac{4}{7}$

2) $\frac{3}{7} - \frac{2}{7} = \frac{1}{7}$

3) $\frac{9}{12} - \frac{3}{12} = \frac{6}{12}$

4) $\frac{8}{10} - \frac{7}{10} = \frac{1}{10}$

5) $\frac{4}{12} - \frac{3}{12} = \frac{1}{12}$

EXERCISE 26

1) $\frac{8}{10} - \frac{4}{10} = \frac{4}{10}$

2) $\frac{3}{11} - \frac{2}{11} = \frac{1}{11}$

3) $\frac{7}{8} - \frac{4}{8} = \frac{3}{8}$

4) $\frac{6}{6} - \frac{1}{6} = \frac{5}{6}$

5) $\frac{5}{9} - \frac{3}{9} = \frac{2}{9}$

EXERCISE 27

1) $\dfrac{2}{5} - \dfrac{1}{5} = \dfrac{1}{5}$

2) $\dfrac{5}{6} - \dfrac{2}{6} = \dfrac{3}{6}$

3) $\dfrac{8}{11} - \dfrac{4}{11} = \dfrac{4}{11}$

4) $\dfrac{2}{3} - \dfrac{1}{3} = \dfrac{1}{3}$

5) $\dfrac{9}{10} - \dfrac{1}{10} = \dfrac{8}{10}$

EXERCISE 28

1) $\dfrac{3}{7} - \dfrac{2}{7} = \dfrac{1}{7}$

2) $\dfrac{9}{12} - \dfrac{4}{12} = \dfrac{5}{12}$

3) $\dfrac{9}{10} - \dfrac{8}{10} = \dfrac{1}{10}$

4) $\dfrac{4}{11} - \dfrac{2}{11} = \dfrac{2}{11}$

5) $\dfrac{11}{11} - \dfrac{9}{11} = \dfrac{2}{11}$

EXERCISE 29

1) $\dfrac{3}{8} - \dfrac{2}{8} = \dfrac{1}{8}$

2) $\dfrac{8}{10} - \dfrac{5}{10} = \dfrac{3}{10}$

3) $\dfrac{3}{6} - \dfrac{2}{6} = \dfrac{1}{6}$

4) $\dfrac{3}{11} - \dfrac{1}{11} = \dfrac{2}{11}$

5) $\dfrac{2}{4} - \dfrac{1}{4} = \dfrac{1}{4}$

6) $\dfrac{4}{9} - \dfrac{2}{9} = \dfrac{2}{9}$

7) $\dfrac{3}{9} - \dfrac{2}{9} = \dfrac{1}{9}$

8) $\dfrac{2}{12} - \dfrac{1}{12} = \dfrac{1}{12}$

9) $\dfrac{2}{10} - \dfrac{1}{10} = \dfrac{1}{10}$

10) $\dfrac{5}{12} - \dfrac{1}{12} = \dfrac{4}{12}$

EXERCISE 30

1) $\dfrac{9}{11} - \dfrac{6}{11} = \dfrac{3}{11}$

2) $\dfrac{2}{12} - \dfrac{1}{12} = \dfrac{1}{12}$

3) $\dfrac{2}{3} - \dfrac{1}{3} = \dfrac{1}{3}$

4) $\dfrac{10}{11} - \dfrac{8}{11} = \dfrac{2}{11}$

5) $\dfrac{5}{9} - \dfrac{1}{9} = \dfrac{4}{9}$

6) $\dfrac{3}{4} - \dfrac{2}{4} = \dfrac{1}{4}$

7) $\dfrac{2}{10} - \dfrac{1}{10} = \dfrac{1}{10}$

8) $\dfrac{4}{7} - \dfrac{2}{7} = \dfrac{2}{7}$

9) $\dfrac{2}{5} - \dfrac{1}{5} = \dfrac{1}{5}$

10) $\dfrac{4}{12} - \dfrac{3}{12} = \dfrac{1}{12}$

EXERCISE 31

1) $\frac{9}{12} - \frac{3}{12} = \frac{6}{12}$

2) $\frac{3}{10} - \frac{1}{10} = \frac{2}{10}$

3) $\frac{2}{10} - \frac{1}{10} = \frac{1}{10}$

4) $\frac{8}{9} - \frac{5}{9} = \frac{3}{9}$

5) $\frac{2}{3} - \frac{1}{3} = \frac{1}{3}$

6) $\frac{9}{12} - \frac{7}{12} = \frac{2}{12}$

7) $\frac{5}{9} - \frac{2}{9} = \frac{3}{9}$

8) $\frac{2}{6} - \frac{1}{6} = \frac{1}{6}$

9) $\frac{2}{5} - \frac{1}{5} = \frac{1}{5}$

10) $\frac{3}{4} - \frac{1}{4} = \frac{2}{4}$

EXERCISE 32

1) $\frac{2}{5} - \frac{1}{5} = \frac{1}{5}$

2) $\frac{6}{11} - \frac{5}{11} = \frac{1}{11}$

3) $\frac{4}{12} - \frac{1}{12} = \frac{3}{12}$

4) $\frac{9}{12} - \frac{2}{12} = \frac{7}{12}$

5) $\frac{7}{10} - \frac{5}{10} = \frac{2}{10}$

6) $\frac{6}{9} - \frac{5}{9} = \frac{1}{9}$

7) $\frac{2}{3} - \frac{1}{3} = \frac{1}{3}$

8) $\frac{3}{12} - \frac{2}{12} = \frac{1}{12}$

9) $\frac{2}{4} - \frac{1}{4} = \frac{1}{4}$

10) $\frac{4}{10} - \frac{2}{10} = \frac{2}{10}$

EXERCISE 33

1) $\frac{3}{4} - \frac{2}{4} = \frac{1}{4}$

2) $\frac{9}{12} - \frac{8}{12} = \frac{1}{12}$

3) $\frac{2}{6} - \frac{1}{6} = \frac{1}{6}$

4) $\frac{4}{5} - \frac{2}{5} = \frac{2}{5}$

5) $\frac{8}{9} - \frac{5}{9} = \frac{3}{9}$

6) $\frac{2}{3} - \frac{1}{3} = \frac{1}{3}$

7) $\frac{2}{11} - \frac{1}{11} = \frac{1}{11}$

8) $\frac{3}{8} - \frac{2}{8} = \frac{1}{8}$

9) $\frac{5}{7} - \frac{1}{7} = \frac{4}{7}$

10) $\frac{8}{12} - \frac{1}{12} = \frac{7}{12}$

EXERCISE 34

1) $\frac{8}{10} - \frac{1}{4} = \frac{16}{20} - \frac{5}{20} = \frac{11}{20}$

2) $\frac{6}{10} - \frac{1}{2} = \frac{6}{10} - \frac{5}{10} = \frac{1}{10}$

3) $\frac{4}{5} - \frac{1}{2} = \frac{8}{10} - \frac{5}{10} = \frac{3}{10}$

4) $\frac{2}{4} - \frac{1}{5} = \frac{10}{20} - \frac{4}{20} = \frac{6}{20} = \frac{3}{10}$

5) $\frac{7}{10} - \frac{1}{3} = \frac{21}{30} - \frac{10}{30} = \frac{11}{30}$

6) $\frac{1}{3} - \frac{1}{4} = \frac{4}{12} - \frac{3}{12} = \frac{1}{12}$

7) $\frac{7}{10} - \frac{1}{2} = \frac{7}{10} - \frac{5}{10} = \frac{2}{10} = \frac{1}{5}$

8) $\frac{1}{2} - \frac{1}{3} = \frac{3}{6} - \frac{2}{6} = \frac{1}{6}$

9) $\frac{3}{4} - \frac{1}{2} = \frac{3}{4} - \frac{2}{4} = \frac{1}{4}$

10) $\frac{1}{2} - \frac{1}{3} = \frac{3}{6} - \frac{2}{6} = \frac{1}{6}$

EXERCISE 35

1) $\frac{3}{4} - \frac{2}{3} = \quad \frac{9}{12} - \frac{8}{12} = \quad \frac{1}{12}$

2) $\frac{2}{4} - \frac{4}{10} = \quad \frac{10}{20} - \frac{8}{20} = \quad \frac{2}{20} = \quad \frac{1}{10}$

3) $\frac{3}{4} - \frac{1}{2} = \quad \frac{3}{4} - \frac{2}{4} = \quad \frac{1}{4}$

4) $\frac{1}{2} - \frac{1}{3} = \quad \frac{3}{6} - \frac{2}{6} = \quad \frac{1}{6}$

5) $\frac{1}{4} - \frac{1}{5} = \quad \frac{5}{20} - \frac{4}{20} = \quad \frac{1}{20}$

6) $\frac{6}{10} - \frac{2}{5} = \quad \frac{6}{10} - \frac{4}{10} = \quad \frac{2}{10} = \quad \frac{1}{5}$

7) $\frac{1}{2} - \frac{1}{4} = \quad \frac{2}{4} - \frac{1}{4} = \quad \frac{1}{4}$

8) $\frac{1}{2} - \frac{1}{3} = \quad \frac{3}{6} - \frac{2}{6} = \quad \frac{1}{6}$

9) $\frac{2}{3} - \frac{1}{2} = \quad \frac{4}{6} - \frac{3}{6} = \quad \frac{1}{6}$

10) $\frac{3}{10} - \frac{1}{5} = \quad \frac{3}{10} - \frac{2}{10} = \quad \frac{1}{10}$

EXERCISE 36

1) $\frac{3}{5} - \frac{1}{4} = \quad \frac{12}{20} - \frac{5}{20} = \quad \frac{7}{20}$

2) $\frac{2}{3} - \frac{1}{2} = \quad \frac{4}{6} - \frac{3}{6} = \quad \frac{1}{6}$

3) $\frac{1}{2} - \frac{2}{5} = \quad \frac{5}{10} - \frac{4}{10} = \quad \frac{1}{10}$

4) $\frac{1}{2} - \frac{2}{5} = \quad \frac{5}{10} - \frac{4}{10} = \quad \frac{1}{10}$

5) $\frac{3}{5} - \frac{1}{2} = \quad \frac{6}{10} - \frac{5}{10} = \quad \frac{1}{10}$

6) $\frac{1}{4} - \frac{1}{5} = \quad \frac{5}{20} - \frac{4}{20} = \quad \frac{1}{20}$

7) $\frac{2}{3} - \frac{2}{5} = \quad \frac{10}{15} - \frac{6}{15} = \quad \frac{4}{15}$

8) $\frac{9}{10} - \frac{2}{5} = \quad \frac{9}{10} - \frac{4}{10} = \quad \frac{5}{10} = \quad \frac{1}{2}$

9) $\frac{2}{3} - \frac{1}{2} = \quad \frac{4}{6} - \frac{3}{6} = \quad \frac{1}{6}$

10) $\frac{2}{3} - \frac{2}{4} = \quad \frac{8}{12} - \frac{6}{12} = \quad \frac{2}{12} = \quad \frac{1}{6}$

EXERCISE 37

1) $\frac{2}{3} - \frac{1}{5} = \quad \frac{10}{15} - \frac{3}{15} = \quad \frac{7}{15}$

2) $\frac{1}{3} - \frac{1}{4} = \quad \frac{4}{12} - \frac{3}{12} = \quad \frac{1}{12}$

3) $\frac{2}{5} - \frac{1}{3} = \quad \frac{6}{15} - \frac{5}{15} = \quad \frac{1}{15}$

4) $\frac{3}{4} - \frac{1}{10} = \quad \frac{15}{20} - \frac{2}{20} = \quad \frac{13}{20}$

5) $\frac{1}{5} - \frac{1}{10} = \quad \frac{2}{10} - \frac{1}{10} = \quad \frac{1}{10}$

6) $\frac{3}{5} - \frac{5}{10} = \quad \frac{6}{10} - \frac{5}{10} = \quad \frac{1}{10}$

7) $\frac{1}{2} - \frac{1}{3} = \quad \frac{3}{6} - \frac{2}{6} = \quad \frac{1}{6}$

8) $\frac{9}{10} - \frac{1}{2} = \quad \frac{9}{10} - \frac{5}{10} = \quad \frac{4}{10} = \quad \frac{2}{5}$

9) $\frac{2}{3} - \frac{1}{10} = \quad \frac{20}{30} - \frac{3}{30} = \quad \frac{17}{30}$

10) $\frac{8}{10} - \frac{1}{4} = \quad \frac{16}{20} - \frac{5}{20} = \quad \frac{11}{20}$

EXERCISE 38

1) $\frac{6}{8} - \frac{8}{16} = \quad \frac{12}{16} - \frac{8}{16} = \quad \frac{4}{16} = \quad \frac{1}{4}$

2) $\frac{8}{12} - \frac{1}{8} = \quad \frac{16}{24} - \frac{3}{24} = \quad \frac{13}{24}$

3) $\frac{8}{14} - \frac{2}{7} = \quad \frac{8}{14} - \frac{4}{14} = \quad \frac{4}{14} = \quad \frac{2}{7}$

4) $\frac{10}{30} - \frac{1}{3} = \quad \frac{10}{30} - \frac{10}{30} = \quad 0$

5) $\frac{4}{6} - \frac{4}{8} = \quad \frac{16}{24} - \frac{12}{24} = \quad \frac{4}{24} = \quad \frac{1}{6}$

6) $\frac{4}{7} - \frac{9}{21} = \quad \frac{12}{21} - \frac{9}{21} = \quad \frac{3}{21} = \quad \frac{1}{7}$

7) $\frac{5}{9} - \frac{1}{3} = \quad \frac{5}{9} - \frac{3}{9} = \quad \frac{2}{9}$

8) $\frac{2}{3} - \frac{5}{18} = \quad \frac{12}{18} - \frac{5}{18} = \quad \frac{7}{18}$

9) $\frac{7}{15} - \frac{2}{6} = \quad \frac{14}{30} - \frac{10}{30} = \quad \frac{4}{30} = \quad \frac{2}{15}$

10) $\frac{8}{28} - \frac{1}{14} = \quad \frac{8}{28} - \frac{2}{28} = \quad \frac{6}{28} = \quad \frac{3}{14}$

EXERCISE 39

1) $\frac{4}{16} - \frac{1}{8} =$ $\frac{4}{16} - \frac{2}{16} =$ $\frac{2}{16} =$ $\frac{1}{8}$

2) $\frac{12}{16} - \frac{5}{8} =$ $\frac{12}{16} - \frac{10}{16} =$ $\frac{2}{16} =$ $\frac{1}{8}$

3) $\frac{3}{4} - \frac{5}{24} =$ $\frac{18}{24} - \frac{5}{24} =$ $\frac{13}{24}$

4) $\frac{7}{11} - \frac{10}{22} =$ $\frac{14}{22} - \frac{10}{22} =$ $\frac{4}{22} =$ $\frac{2}{11}$

5) $\frac{2}{6} - \frac{3}{18} =$ $\frac{6}{18} - \frac{3}{18} =$ $\frac{3}{18} =$ $\frac{1}{6}$

6) $\frac{5}{7} - \frac{10}{28} =$ $\frac{20}{28} - \frac{10}{28} =$ $\frac{10}{28} =$ $\frac{5}{14}$

7) $\frac{4}{11} - \frac{7}{22} =$ $\frac{8}{22} - \frac{7}{22} =$ $\frac{1}{22}$

8) $\frac{12}{14} - \frac{1}{28} =$ $\frac{24}{28} - \frac{1}{28} =$ $\frac{23}{28}$

9) $\frac{2}{3} - \frac{6}{18} =$ $\frac{12}{18} - \frac{6}{18} =$ $\frac{6}{18} =$ $\frac{1}{3}$

10) $\frac{1}{9} - \frac{1}{27} =$ $\frac{3}{27} - \frac{1}{27} =$ $\frac{2}{27}$

EXERCISE 40

1) $\frac{3}{4} - \frac{4}{14} =$ $\frac{21}{28} - \frac{8}{28} =$ $\frac{13}{28}$

2) $\frac{2}{6} - \frac{3}{15} =$ $\frac{10}{30} - \frac{6}{30} =$ $\frac{4}{30} =$ $\frac{2}{15}$

3) $\frac{5}{13} - \frac{9}{26} =$ $\frac{10}{26} - \frac{9}{26} =$ $\frac{1}{26}$

4) $\frac{3}{5} - \frac{4}{30} =$ $\frac{18}{30} - \frac{4}{30} =$ $\frac{14}{30} =$ $\frac{7}{15}$

5) $\frac{5}{12} - \frac{1}{4} =$ $\frac{5}{12} - \frac{3}{12} =$ $\frac{2}{12} =$ $\frac{1}{6}$

6) $\frac{6}{14} - \frac{3}{7} =$ $\frac{6}{14} - \frac{6}{14} =$ 0

7) $\frac{6}{7} - \frac{5}{21} =$ $\frac{18}{21} - \frac{5}{21} =$ $\frac{13}{21}$

8) $\frac{4}{6} - \frac{11}{24} =$ $\frac{16}{24} - \frac{11}{24} =$ $\frac{5}{24}$

9) $\frac{8}{14} - \frac{1}{28} =$ $\frac{16}{28} - \frac{1}{28} =$ $\frac{15}{28}$

10) $\frac{4}{11} - \frac{3}{22} =$ $\frac{8}{22} - \frac{3}{22} =$ $\frac{5}{22}$

EXERCISE 41

1) $9\frac{1}{3} - 2\frac{1}{4} =$ $9\frac{4}{12} - 2\frac{3}{12} =$ $7\frac{1}{12}$

2) $8\frac{1}{3} - 3\frac{1}{5} =$ $8\frac{5}{15} - 3\frac{3}{15} =$ $5\frac{2}{15}$

3) $8\frac{1}{2} - 2\frac{3}{10} =$ $8\frac{5}{10} - 2\frac{3}{10} =$ $6\frac{2}{10} =$ $6\frac{1}{5}$

4) $5\frac{2}{4} - 3\frac{2}{10} =$ $5\frac{10}{20} - 3\frac{4}{20} =$ $2\frac{6}{20} =$ $2\frac{3}{10}$

5) $9\frac{2}{5} - 1\frac{3}{10} =$ $9\frac{4}{10} - 1\frac{3}{10} =$ $8\frac{1}{10}$

6) $5\frac{1}{2} - 2\frac{2}{10} =$ $5\frac{5}{10} - 2\frac{2}{10} =$ $3\frac{3}{10}$

7) $9\frac{4}{5} - 2\frac{1}{3} =$ $9\frac{12}{15} - 2\frac{5}{15} =$ $7\frac{7}{15}$

8) $6\frac{3}{4} - 2\frac{3}{5} =$ $6\frac{15}{20} - 2\frac{12}{20} =$ $4\frac{3}{20}$

9) $9\frac{9}{10} - 3\frac{1}{3} =$ $9\frac{27}{30} - 3\frac{10}{30} =$ $6\frac{17}{30}$

0) $7\frac{3}{4} - 3\frac{1}{5} =$ $7\frac{15}{20} - 3\frac{4}{20} =$ $4\frac{11}{20}$

EXERCISE 42

1) $7\frac{8}{10} - 3\frac{1}{3} =$ $7\frac{24}{30} - 3\frac{10}{30} =$ $4\frac{14}{30} =$ $4\frac{7}{15}$

2) $8\frac{4}{5} - 1\frac{1}{3} =$ $8\frac{12}{15} - 1\frac{5}{15} =$ $7\frac{7}{15}$

3) $8\frac{2}{3} - 4\frac{1}{5} =$ $8\frac{10}{15} - 4\frac{3}{15} =$ $4\frac{7}{15}$

4) $8\frac{1}{2} - 3\frac{1}{10} =$ $8\frac{5}{10} - 3\frac{1}{10} =$ $5\frac{4}{10} =$ $5\frac{2}{5}$

5) $6\frac{1}{2} - 2\frac{2}{5} =$ $6\frac{5}{10} - 2\frac{4}{10} =$ $4\frac{1}{10}$

6) $9\frac{3}{5} - 4\frac{6}{10} =$ $9\frac{6}{10} - 4\frac{6}{10} =$ 5

7) $7\frac{2}{3} - 2\frac{1}{4} =$ $7\frac{8}{12} - 2\frac{3}{12} =$ $5\frac{5}{12}$

8) $7\frac{2}{4} - 1\frac{1}{3} =$ $7\frac{6}{12} - 1\frac{4}{12} =$ $6\frac{2}{12} =$ $6\frac{1}{6}$

9) $5\frac{1}{3} - 2\frac{3}{10} =$ $5\frac{10}{30} - 2\frac{9}{30} =$ $3\frac{1}{30}$

0) $9\frac{1}{2} - 3\frac{1}{4} =$ $9\frac{2}{4} - 3\frac{1}{4} =$ $6\frac{1}{4}$

EXERCISE 43

1) $6\frac{2}{4} - 1\frac{1}{2} = \quad 6\frac{2}{4} - 1\frac{2}{4} = \quad 5$

2) $6\frac{1}{3} - 2\frac{1}{5} = \quad 6\frac{5}{15} - 2\frac{3}{15} = \quad 4\frac{2}{15}$

3) $7\frac{4}{5} - 4\frac{3}{10} = \quad 7\frac{8}{10} - 4\frac{3}{10} = \quad 3\frac{5}{10} = \quad 3\frac{1}{2}$

4) $6\frac{3}{5} - 4\frac{1}{3} = \quad 6\frac{9}{15} - 4\frac{5}{15} = \quad 2\frac{4}{15}$

5) $5\frac{3}{4} - 1\frac{1}{5} = \quad 5\frac{15}{20} - 1\frac{4}{20} = \quad 4\frac{11}{20}$

6) $7\frac{1}{2} - 2\frac{2}{10} = \quad 7\frac{5}{10} - 2\frac{2}{10} = \quad 5\frac{3}{10}$

7) $8\frac{3}{4} - 1\frac{2}{3} = \quad 8\frac{9}{12} - 1\frac{8}{12} = \quad 7\frac{1}{12}$

8) $7\frac{3}{4} - 1\frac{2}{3} = \quad 7\frac{9}{12} - 1\frac{8}{12} = \quad 6\frac{1}{12}$

9) $8\frac{3}{4} - 2\frac{1}{2} = \quad 8\frac{3}{4} - 2\frac{2}{4} = \quad 6\frac{1}{4}$

0) $8\frac{3}{4} - 3\frac{1}{2} = \quad 8\frac{3}{4} - 3\frac{2}{4} = \quad 5\frac{1}{4}$

EXERCISE 44

1) $9\frac{1}{2} - 3\frac{1}{3} = \quad 9\frac{3}{6} - 3\frac{2}{6} = \quad 6\frac{1}{6}$

2) $8\frac{8}{10} - 1\frac{2}{3} = \quad 8\frac{24}{30} - 1\frac{20}{30} = \quad 7\frac{4}{30} = \quad 7\frac{2}{15}$

3) $5\frac{2}{3} - 3\frac{1}{5} = \quad 5\frac{10}{15} - 3\frac{3}{15} = \quad 2\frac{7}{15}$

4) $8\frac{3}{4} - 1\frac{1}{10} = \quad 8\frac{15}{20} - 1\frac{2}{20} = \quad 7\frac{13}{20}$

5) $7\frac{2}{4} - 2\frac{2}{5} = \quad 7\frac{10}{20} - 2\frac{8}{20} = \quad 5\frac{2}{20} = \quad 5\frac{1}{10}$

6) $5\frac{3}{4} - 3\frac{1}{2} = \quad 5\frac{3}{4} - 3\frac{2}{4} = \quad 2\frac{1}{4}$

7) $7\frac{1}{2} - 4\frac{2}{10} = \quad 7\frac{5}{10} - 4\frac{2}{10} = \quad 3\frac{3}{10}$

8) $6\frac{4}{5} - 4\frac{2}{3} = \quad 6\frac{12}{15} - 4\frac{10}{15} = \quad 2\frac{2}{15}$

9) $7\frac{9}{10} - 2\frac{1}{2} = \quad 7\frac{9}{10} - 2\frac{5}{10} = \quad 5\frac{4}{10} = \quad 5\frac{2}{5}$

0) $5\frac{4}{5} - 1\frac{2}{3} = \quad 5\frac{12}{15} - 1\frac{10}{15} = \quad 4\frac{2}{15}$

EXERCISE 45

1) $6\frac{1}{4} - 1\frac{1}{5} = \quad 6\frac{5}{20} - 1\frac{4}{20} = \quad 5\frac{1}{20}$

2) $8\frac{2}{3} - 3\frac{2}{4} = \quad 8\frac{8}{12} - 3\frac{6}{12} = \quad 5\frac{2}{12} = \quad 5\frac{1}{6}$

3) $6\frac{3}{4} - 3\frac{7}{10} = \quad 6\frac{15}{20} - 3\frac{14}{20} = \quad 3\frac{1}{20}$

4) $6\frac{2}{3} - 1\frac{1}{5} = \quad 6\frac{10}{15} - 1\frac{3}{15} = \quad 5\frac{7}{15}$

5) $6\frac{2}{4} - 2\frac{1}{5} = \quad 6\frac{10}{20} - 2\frac{4}{20} = \quad 4\frac{6}{20} = \quad 4\frac{3}{10}$

6) $9\frac{2}{5} - 4\frac{1}{3} = \quad 9\frac{6}{15} - 4\frac{5}{15} = \quad 5\frac{1}{15}$

7) $9\frac{2}{3} - 3\frac{1}{5} = \quad 9\frac{10}{15} - 3\frac{3}{15} = \quad 6\frac{7}{15}$

8) $8\frac{1}{2} - 2\frac{1}{4} = \quad 8\frac{2}{4} - 2\frac{1}{4} = \quad 6\frac{1}{4}$

9) $5\frac{1}{4} - 3\frac{1}{10} = \quad 5\frac{5}{20} - 3\frac{2}{20} = \quad 2\frac{3}{20}$

0) $5\frac{3}{4} - 2\frac{1}{2} = \quad 5\frac{3}{4} - 2\frac{2}{4} = \quad 3\frac{1}{4}$

EXERCISE 46

1) $7\frac{3}{4} - 4\frac{2}{5} = \quad 7\frac{15}{20} - 4\frac{8}{20} = \quad 3\frac{7}{20}$

2) $7\frac{3}{4} - 1\frac{1}{2} = \quad 7\frac{3}{4} - 1\frac{2}{4} = \quad 6\frac{1}{4}$

3) $6\frac{1}{2} - 4\frac{1}{10} = \quad 6\frac{5}{10} - 4\frac{1}{10} = \quad 2\frac{4}{10} = \quad 2\frac{2}{5}$

4) $6\frac{3}{4} - 3\frac{2}{3} = \quad 6\frac{9}{12} - 3\frac{8}{12} = \quad 3\frac{1}{12}$

5) $8\frac{1}{3} - 3\frac{1}{4} = \quad 8\frac{4}{12} - 3\frac{3}{12} = \quad 5\frac{1}{12}$

6) $7\frac{1}{2} - 3\frac{2}{5} = \quad 7\frac{5}{10} - 3\frac{4}{10} = \quad 4\frac{1}{10}$

7) $9\frac{1}{2} - 4\frac{1}{3} = \quad 9\frac{3}{6} - 4\frac{2}{6} = \quad 5\frac{1}{6}$

8) $9\frac{2}{3} - 3\frac{1}{5} = \quad 9\frac{10}{15} - 3\frac{3}{15} = \quad 6\frac{7}{15}$

9) $9\frac{4}{5} - 3\frac{2}{4} = \quad 9\frac{16}{20} - 3\frac{10}{20} = \quad 6\frac{6}{20} = \quad 6\frac{3}{10}$

0) $6\frac{1}{2} - 3\frac{1}{3} = \quad 6\frac{3}{6} - 3\frac{2}{6} = \quad 3\frac{1}{6}$

Made in the USA
Las Vegas, NV
03 July 2024

91824784R00040